Love's
Little Instruction Book

———————♥———————

Love's
Little Instruction Book

Romantic Hints for Lovers of All Ages

Annie Pigeon

Pinnacle Books
Windsor Publishing Corp.

PINNACLE BOOKS are published by

Windsor Publishing Corp.
475 Park Avenue South
New York, NY 10016

The P logo Reg. U.S. Pat. & TM Off. Pinnacle is a trademark of Windsor Publishing Corp.

Second Printing: February, 1996

Printed in the United States of America

To Smush from Smeesh.

1. Ask her mother to dance.

♥

2. Remember his parents' birthdays.

♥

3. Share the remote control.

♥

4. Hang baby pictures of the two of you side by side over the bed.

♥

5. Put smiley faces on the pancakes.

♥

6. Never say, "You got the jar open because I loosened it up for you."

♥

7. Never say, "You sound just like your mother."

♥

8. Never agree that she needs to lose five pounds.

♥

9. Tie her shoes when she's too pregnant to bend.

♥

10. Leave a love message on the answering machine.

♥

11. Say thank you for small favors.

♥

12. Send a love fax.

♥

13. Fill a "feel better" jar with paper slips noting reasons why you love each other.

♥

14. Give each other coupons redeemable for back rubs.

♥

15. Put the toilet seat down.

♥

16. Don't make him stop for directions.

♥

17. Flatulence happens.

♥

18. PMS happens.

♥

19. Take turns being irrational.

♥

20. Don't try to solve more than one problem
at a time.

♥
21. Don't whine.

♥
22. Don't gloat.

♥
23. Don't nag.

♥
24. Don't open each other's mail.

♥

25. Don't throw out his favorite old clothes.

♥

26. Be silent when his plan doesn't work.

♥

27. Talk him out of the hair weave.

♥

28. Talk her out of the nose job.

♥

29. Agree he looks *great* in the pink paisley tie.

♥

30. Don't bring home fudge when she's on a diet.

♥

31. Phone when you're running late.

♥

32. Have his car waxed.

♥

33. Feed his fish.

♥

34. Chat with her plants.

♥

35. Turn down the blankets and put a candy on the pillow.

♥

36. Sign up for tango lessons.

♥

37. Don't eat the last chocolate chip cookie.

♥

38. Don't beat him to the punch line.

♥

39. Don't return each other's gifts.

♥

40. Fall asleep holding hands.

♥

41. Wake him up with a kiss.

♥

42. Have a TV-off night once a week.

♥

43. Turn off the phone ringer.

♥

44. Serve heart-shaped waffles.

♥

45. Bring home a balloon.

♥

46. Make her birthday a week-long festival.

♥

47. Buy extravagant sheets.

♥

48. Start a joint bank account.

♥

49. Go with him to the Stallone movie.

♥

50. Go with her to the Mel Gibson movie.

♥

51. Compare his behind favorably with Mel Gibson's.

52. Compare her shape favorably with Cindy Crawford's.

♥

53. Leave a love note on the bathroom mirror.

♥

54. Let him watch Formula One.

♥

55. Don't remind him of the last thing he did wrong.

♥

56. Bring home one rose.

♥

57. Gas up the car.

♥

58. Don't tell her when it's a bad hair day.

♥

59. Don't offer to measure his bald spot.

♥

60. Send a singing telegram.

♥

61. Keep a secret stash for buying gifts.

♥

62. Send her lace lingerie.

♥

63. Buy him silk boxer shorts.

♥

64. Don't sit in his favorite chair.

♥

65. Ask for his help when you don't need it.

♥

66. Watch his cholesterol.

♥

67. Cut back on fats together.

♥

68. Reminisce about the day you met.

♥

69. Sing oldies in the car.

♥

70. Snuggle under a beach umbrella.

♥

71. Burn real firewood.

♥

72. Get up with the baby when it's not your turn.

♥

73. Share diaper duty.

♥

74. Let him think it was his idea.

♥

75. Use candlelight.

♥

76. Take a couples massage class.

♥

77. Jog slowly enough so he can keep up.

♥

78. Rub ice on her neck in a heat wave.

♥

79. Tickle.

♥

80. Wink.

♥

81. Don't flirt with her best friend.

♥

82. Don't flirt with his worst enemy.

♥

83. Send flowers when there's no occasion.

♥

84. Say something in French.

♥

85. Ride the ferris wheel.

♥

86. Let her choose the wine.

♥

87. Let him choose the wallpaper.

♥

88. Let him win at Scrabble.

♥

89. Find her sister a date.

♥

90. Remind him to take his vitamins.

♥

91. Buy her a lottery ticket.

♥

92. Play her birthday on the roulette wheel.

♥

93. If she spent all day cooking it, compliment it.

♥

94. Ask his mother for his favorite recipe.

♥

95. Share your entrées.

♥

96. Share a sundae.

♥

97. Oven mitts are not a gift.

♥

98. Hedge trimmers are not a gift.

♥

99. Leaving it in the shopping bag is not gift wrapping.

♥

100. A belated gift is better than no gift at all.

♥

101. If you promised, do it.

♥

102. Don't hide when he gets out the camera.

♥

103. Keep a savings account just for vacations.

♥

104. Frequent a country inn.

♥

105. Be punctual.

♥

106. Don't ask him to buy your mascara.

♥

107. Don't use his razor on your legs.

♥

108. When she makes Beef Wellington, don't ask
for ketchup.

♥

109. Wear the chartreuse sweater she knit you.

♥

110. Don't miss a spot with that sunscreen.

♥

111. Don't grind his gears.

♥

112. Show interest in each other's hobbies.

♥

113. Remember, she drinks *diet* soda.

♥

114. Don't let him teach you to drive.

♥

115. Praise his ship in a bottle.

♥

116. Hide a love note in his briefcase.

♥

117. Hide a love note in his briefs.

♥

118. Try your hand at a sonnet.

♥

119. Use pet names.

♥

120. Don't have him paged by his pet name at work.

♥

121. Meet her at the airport.

♥

122. Pick him up when his car is in the shop.

♥

123. Plan a surprise getaway weekend.

♥

124. Don't make the waiters sing him Happy Birthday.

♥

125. Don't let her go to her surprise party without makeup.

126. Don't make fat jokes when she's pregnant.

♥

127. Go with her to Lamaze class.

♥

128. Don't faint in the delivery room.

♥

129. Make up before bed, or in it.

♥

130. So what if she can't carry a tune.

♥

131. So what if he can't work the VCR.

♥

132. Don't say "You'll never understand."

♥

133. Don't say "Your family is plotting against me."

♥

134. Chocolate is always welcome.

♥

135. Fan him on a hot day.

♥

136. Offer to peel her grapes.

♥

137. Offer to carry her over a puddle.

♥

138. Open the car door for her.

♥

139. Plant a tree together.

♥

140. Tell her mother she raised a wonderful daughter.

♥

141. Tell his mother she raised a perfect son.

♥

142. Tell her she looks great in the swimsuit.

♥

143. Whisper sweet somethings.

♥

144. Let him order the anchovies.

♥

145. So what if she has cellulite.

♥

146. So what if he has love handles.

♥

147. Whistle at her.

♥
148. Goose him.
♥
149. Nuzzle.
♥
150. Cuddle.
♥
151. Stroke.
♥

152. Joke.

♥

153. Take a Jacuzzi.

♥

154. Tell her she's extraordinary.

♥

155. Babysit his monster nephew.

♥

156. Buy him a subscription to his favorite magazine.

♥

157. Take a horse and buggy ride.

♥

158. Neck in the back of a taxi.

♥

159. Tell him when he has milk on his mustache.

♥

160. Tell her when she has lipstick on her teeth.

♥

161. Quarrels happen.

♥

162. Everyone has an off night sometimes.

♥

163. Charm his boss.

♥

164. Wash each other's hair.

♥

165. Tell him you wouldn't trade him for anyone.

♥

166. Never go crazy simultaneously.

♥

167. Go through the revolving door together.

♥

168. Don't hold a grudge.

♥

169. Don't complain about him to your friends.

♥

170. Feel his biceps.

♥

171. Name a stuffed animal after him.

♥

172. Have her horoscope done.

♥

173. Have his caricature done.

♥

174. Get him a heating pad.

♥

175. Name a boat after her.

♥

176. Ride a bicycle built for two.

♥

177. Propose toasts to each other.

♥

178. Let him tell how he got his high school letter—again.

♥

179. Tell him you're glad your first love moved to Omaha.

♥

180. Assure her she's much prettier than your secretary.

181. Always bring a small gift home from a business trip.

♥

182. Don't ask her to "hold it in" during a car trip.

♥

183. Pay her parking ticket.

♥

184. Clip coupons together.

♥

185. Look sharp for her high school reunion.

♥

186. Join her father for golf.

♥

187. Use that Nordic Track she bought you.

♥

188. Don't mention the favors you've done
each other.

♥

189. Don't point out the dustbunnies.

♥

190. Respect his car.

♥

191. Let him kiss you when his beard is stubbly.

♥

192. Don't make fun of her clay facial mask.

♥

193. Be generous.

♥

194. Fluff his pillow.

♥

195. Make time for each other.

♥

196. Roast her a marshmallow.

♥

197. Adopt a pet together.

♥

198. Rent *Two For the Road*.

♥

199. Rent *Sabrina*.

♥

200. Rent *Roman Holiday*.

♥

201. Play strip tease poker.

♥

202. Wear matching rings.

203. Find his lost car keys.

♥

204. Find her lost earring.

♥

205. Zip her up.

♥

206. Shoo a spider for her.

♥

207. Wear his favorite perfume.

♥

208. Wear her favorite cologne.

♥

209. Tell each other what you dreamed last night.

♥

210. Share your childhood memories.

♥

211. Confide your hopes.

212. Confess your fears.

213. Give each other the benefit of the doubt.

214. Discourage meddling friends.

215. Hide a love message in a fortune cookie.

216. Don't obsess on imperfections.

♥

217. He's not cheap, he's frugal.

♥

218. He's not lazy, he's relaxed.

♥

219. Don't demand.

♥

220. Don't command.

♥

221. Write your own vows.

♥

222. Lunch at Wendy's is not a wedding reception.

♥

223. Marriage is not a dress rehearsal.

♥

224. Remember, it's for better or worse.

♥

225. Take a ride in a hot air balloon.

♥

226. Ride a ski lift even if you don't ski.

♥

227. Sunrises are more romantic than sunsets.

♥

228. Get her a life-sized stuffed koala bear.

♥

229. Stay home and snuggle on New Year's Eve.

♥

230. So what if Valentine's Day is commercial.

♥

231. Let him carve the turkey.

♥

232. Share the drumsticks.

♥

233. Buy her a pair of lovebirds.

♥

234. Reupholster the loveseat.

♥

235. Don't hog the blankets.

♥

236. Admire his dimple.

♥

237. Be impractical sometimes.

♥

238. Be extravagant sometimes.

♥

239. Be spontaneous often.

♥

240. Get goofy.

♥

241. Only eat garlic as a twosome.

♥

242. Praise his tennis serve.

♥

243. Don't say, "That's not the way it happened."

♥

244. A little Johnny Mathis never hurt.

♥

245. The toilet paper hangs over, not under.

♥

246. Tell him he sings like Sinatra.

♥

247. Tell him he swivels like Elvis.

♥

248. Ennui happens.

♥

249. Faux pas happen.

♥

250. Make new friends together.

♥

251. Root for his favorite teams.

♥

252. Don't spend more than five straight hours in a car together.

♥

253. Share a sleeping bag.

♥

254. Search for shooting stars.

♥

255. An occasional food fight may relieve tension.

♥

256. Bake him a pie.

♥

257. Avoid fixing up your respective best friends.

♥

258. Filing joint tax returns is no day at the beach.

♥

259. Everyone needs some space.

♥

260. Take a nap together.

♥

261. Be sincere.

♥

262. Hug a bunch.

♥

263. Know when to bite your tongue.

♥

264. Not even true love can withstand winter camping.

265. Everyone should pick up a check sometimes.

266. Don't hide the sports section.

267. Sing, hum, or play "your" song.

268. Don't tell her that her colors clash.

269. Read him a racy passage.

♥

270. Volunteer to do a hated chore.

♥

271. Don't compare him to someone "better."

♥

272. Display her photo on your desk.

♥

273. Circle all important dates at the start of each year.

♥

274. Nibble his ear.

♥

275. Never leave home without a peck on the cheek.

♥

276. Don't be a backseat driver.

♥

277. Tell her she's got great legs.

♥

278. Sharpen his pencils.

♥

279. Love isn't always convenient.

♥

280. Conversation doesn't mean waiting for your turn to talk.

♥

281. If it weren't for marriage you'd have to fight with a stranger.

♥

282. Timing isn't everything, but it's a lot.

♥

283. McDonald's is not a night on the town.

♥

284. Make her your beneficiary.

♥

285. Play hookey together.

♥

286. Be naughty together.

♥

287. Serve oysters.

♥

288. Let's hear it for monogamy.

♥

289. Occasional jealousy is flattering.

♥

290. Maintain a balance of power.

♥

291. Your partner is not a mindreader.

♥

292. Tease.

♥

293. Say pretty please.

♥

294. Tell him he's indispensable.

♥

295. Have her watch engraved.

♥

296. If he says tomato, don't say to-mah-to.

♥

297. Blow in her ear.

♥

298. Write love messages on his back with your finger.

♥

299. Diamonds *are* a girl's best friend.

♥

300. No cubic zirconium, please.

♥

301. Ask if she prefers silver or gold.

♥

302. Have your favorite deejay devote
a song to her.

♥

303. Sing a karaoke duet.

♥

304. Take a second honeymoon.

♥

305. Don't do business on your second honeymoon.

♥

306. Pack a picnic for two.

♥

307. Buy her a share of your favorite stock.

♥

308. Share the Sunday paper in bed.

♥

309. Put the Sunday paper back the way you found it.

♥

310. Refold his maps the way you found them.

♥

311. Never say, "Don't muss my hair."

♥

312. Ask him what he'd like you to wear.

♥

313. Take a cruise.

♥

314. Get up early and make the coffee.

♥

315. Ask him how he'd like his eggs.

♥

316. Hold the door open.

♥

317. Encourage his ambitions.

♥

318. Let's hear it for chivalry.

♥

319. Fill her tub with bubbles.

♥

320. Champagne is always welcome.

♥

321. Don't use the last of her hair conditioner.

♥

322. Wash your lipstick off his collar.

♥

323. Admire her yearbook photo.

♥

324. Never stop referring to her as your bride.

♥

325. Once in a while do brunch instead of golf.

♥

326. Once in a while encourage him to play eighteen holes.

♥

327. Attend the Halloween party as Antony and Cleopatra.

♥

328. Attend the Halloween party as Mickey and Minnie.

♥

329. Dust his bowling trophies.

♥

330. He must have good taste, he chose you.

♥

331. If you want to keep him handy, don't treat him as a handyman.

♥

332. Let him look at the bikinis on the beach.

♥

333. Don't get sand in the suntan oil.

♥

334. Tell him the gray hair is distinguished.

♥

335. Buy her a bonsai.

♥

336. At the movies, snuggling is more important than plot.

♥

337. Owning two TVs is cheaper than paying a divorce lawyer.

♥

338. Remodeling is the enemy of romance.

♥

339. Don't confide in his ex-wife.

♥

340. Don't ask for a prenuptial agreement.

♥

341. Don't bring your lawyer on your first date.

♥

342. Show some understanding.

343. Don't go on a tell-all talk show together.

344. Admire his chest hair.

345. Butter his croissant.

346. Rub his temples.

347. Buy her a painting of your honeymoon locale.

♥

348. Squeeze hands during take-offs and landings.

♥

349. Finish each other's sentences.

♥

350. Edit yourself.

♥

351. Be gracious when his relatives drop in unexpectedly.

♥

352. Wear his favorite dress.

♥

353. Don't expect her to cook on your anniversary.

♥

354. Fold each other's laundry.

♥

355. Wear the scarf his grandmother knit for you.

♥

356. Find a place to kiss that you've never kissed before.

♥

357. Take a bath together.

♥

358. Feed each other strawberries and whipped cream.

♥

359. Read some Byron and Shelley.

♥

360. Listen to some Cole Porter.

♥

361. Total honesty is sadistic.

♥

362. Let's hear it for little white lies.

♥

363. Apologize.

♥

364. Compromise.

♥

365. Give a guy a break.